What I

Jeffrey Wainwright was born in 1944 in Stoke-on-Trent, England. He was educated at Longton High School and the University of Leeds, and went on to teach American Literature at the University of Wales and later for a time at Long Island University, Brooklyn, New York. In 1973 he moved to teach at Manchester Metropolitan University, where he became Professor of English and a founding member of the MMU Writing School before retiring in 2008. In 1984 he was Judith Wilson Fellow at St John's College, Cambridge. Wainwright has written many articles and reviews on poetry and two books of criticism, *Poetry the Basics* (3rd edition 2015) and *Acceptable Words: Essays on the Poetry of Geoffrey Hill* (2005), and has translated plays by Péguy, Corneille, Claudel and Koltès for radio and stage. He has been married to Judith Wainwright since 1967, with whom he has two children and four grandchildren. He has travelled extensively in the USA and Australia, and spends parts of the year in Umbria, Italy.

Also by JEFFREY WAINWRIGHT
from Carcanet Press

The Reasoner (2012)

Clarity or Death! (2008)

Out of the Air (1999)

The Red-Headed Pupil (1994)

Selected Poems (1985)

What Must Happen

JEFFREY WAINWRIGHT

CARCANET

for Judith

First published in Great Britain in 2016 by

CARCANET PRESS LIMITED
Alliance House, 30 Cross Street
Manchester M2 7AQ
www.carcanet.co.uk

Text copyright © Jeffrey Wainwright, 2016

A CIP catalogue record for this book is available
from the British Library, ISBN 9781784101961.

The publisher acknowledges financial
assistance from Arts Council England.

Contents

WHAT MUST HAPPEN

What Must Happen

'Funny – to be a Century –
And see the People – going by –'

EMILY DICKINSON

1.

Now all the Sciences of History are at the door,
The World's Reason and his suite,
Long-stirruped, rearing, riding,
Storming the earth and stunning the air.

Look at His Highness there in white and gold,
And this other in his oh-so-modest blue;
Look how their men are drawn to breast the rise –
Accoutred and alive, how historical they are!

The ensign posts away, along the line, along the day,
And at its end happens upon His Majesty,
Sniffling upon a log, and tip-toes on his way.
Two Emperors can be caught with just one bean.

2.

Now all the Sciences of History are at the door
With caps in hand and aprons spread
Crossing themselves and speaking French.
Small fires seize picture frames and chairs.

In *bibliothèque*, café, *platz* and upper room
Prophets and thinkers sniff the visionary smoke,
Number their theses and dress to kill.
Their aeropainting will re-touch the dawn,

Their willing corporals stun and storm,
Their strapped-up martyrs charge and call:
'Fools, did we think we should live forever?
Look how historical the future is!'

3.

Now all the Sciences of History are at the door
And, after a little stun and storm, shock and awe,
Are smiling, shirt-sleeved, making nice: 'May we come in,
May we sit down? Look at our invisible hands –

The latest manicure! – how may they work for you?
We aim to make the world to count
In perfect synchrony, to teach the world to chant:
"There is no past, all things are new, we act: we are."

So just sign where it says: "In none we trust",
And here again, "In none we trust",
And just once more "In none we trust".
How historical you were, and now how free!'

4.

Now all the Sciences of History are at the door
Or tent-flap, fly-screen, wire-entanglement
And peer in. Still on their jotters there's little spilt
Or spattered, and still they will reiterate:

'Time must be History, and History an Idea
Patient of its uncoiling
To an End. Otherwise we fall through,
Like light through glass, nothing now and nothing then.'

Boys on their cots think they hear water
And the clink of tin: in their dreams of whiskers
They will soon be shaved. Wounds get stuck with cat
Or blanket-hair. What must happen, what need not?

Crockery

Antiquarium

He chomps their squirming comrades one in either hand,
but Ulysses gets the Cyclops drunk, lops and sharpens
a mighty pine, has four men lift it and in lock-step drive it
. . . but this is a story you know well enough,

like Ulysses clinging to the ram's belly-fleece,
his toes cinched on the creature's balls and seeming to wink
as he slips by the monster's blinded hands.
But why would anyone want these scenes on a water jar?

Perhaps it's meant to show monstrosity worsted by human nous,
gross voracity outwitted by such as cherish table-ware,
cups and plates, things to hold our water, light and wine,
an arm of the technic that helps us weaklings on our way.

All of it will break in time but it will not rot.
Thus a patient girl with a brush and glue
can find us as we were and – we *can* come this far –
weep for Polyphemus and his bleeding eye.

Etruria Hall

Wedgwood would not put such pain on his own Etruscan ware.
None of his artists was invited in to capture him,
woozy but upright in his chair as he watched Dr Bent
saw through the thickened bone above his knee.

That goes under 'breakages', along with misbegotten
cream-ware he will not back-stamp with his name
but grinds beneath his wooden heel. Hithering and thithering,
mithering on *bucchero* and what art should grace

my lady's table and Portland pots and salesmanship,
he pegs it back by moonlight to Etruria Hall,
his mind turning on the cogs of betterment as he goes,
fresh glazes, firings and the smooth runnings of his new canal.

From the clay-end to St Martin's Lane everything is canalised:
the mould-maker, pugman, dipper, paintress, gilder, fireman,
sagger-maker, placer, drawer, all in work,
all provided for in New Etruria's commodious light.

Dirt

Window-nets are tell-tales. Idleness will not survive
the war with dirt. So she's on her hands and knees
to stone the doorstep, then the window-sill;
the sweeping of your bricks shows you what you are.

Dust slides in unseen onto mantelpiece and rug.
Collars starched for Sunday-best are smirched by noon –
wash your neck, wash your neck – dolly-peg and mangle
until at last the liberations of Electrolux.

Deep-breathing by an open window, sanatorium-style,
is recommended, but dirt still settles in the phlegm,
bronchitic thickenings, spitting in the street, the scourings
of flint and soft soot pocketed by the hapless lung.

The paintress of majolica licked her brush and died.
Dippers lined their guts with milk and Epsom salts
to no avail. God bless the Factory Acts
that saved my mother from the leaded glaze!

China Cabinet

The most delicate of porcelain is made by angry fire.
The magma of manufactory, Vesuvial spits, globs and drops,
imitating how the earth made itself
from a belly of entombed or tunnelled flame.

And it creates this wasp-waisted girl in crinolines,
cheeks just ablush, slim fingers offering a posy
of forget-me-nots for their ceramic scent,
her slipper cool enough to step on ice.

Soon she shall have her spaniel and her swain,
Jemima Puddleduck and Mr Fox for company,
he in knee-breeches and frock coat, hands behind his back
looking most lawyerly as he inclines to listen in.

This is her domain where she can breathe air
as un-flecked as her gown. Live here my lady,
safe from all that muck outside:
you are the beauty we have come to know.

Homus Economicus

And thousands of 'em sold, these gentle and
respectful maids, their blushes packed in straw,
all entrusted to the slow canals, just as Etruscan potters
sent their stuff down the Tiber to the mouth of Rome.

Homus economicus, dragging from the local quag
a tea-service to Queen Charlotte's taste;
mollifying 'fat housewives' who want their ware
more or less 'yallower Mr Wagwood, *if you will.*'

'Stout classicist', entrepreneur of grave-goods,
always testing novelty: black figure, red figure,
Venus modelled against a choice of blue, black, lilac,
sage-green or any manganese that can be found.

Then he's liberation's honourable fashionista:
his medallion of the kneeling slave in jasper-ware –
'*Am I not a man and a brother?*' – soon *à la mode*
as tea-caddies, hair-pins, bracelets. Thousands of 'em sold.

Going Global

Smithereened along with Royal Art,
I doubt our old cow-butter can be found
among the world's new earthenware. China
comes from China, as it may, my lady from Brazil.

Like them, our folk left the one-egg farms for work.
Now, as then, cities grow like marrows in the wet:
shanties and dormitories rigged, showrooms lacquered.
Backache. Repeat. Silica. Repeat. Breathing. Repeat.

Breathing... Do they do this better than was managed then?
In infant death for instance: Longton
in 1899 – 327 per 1000.
And how many years are the median now? > 46? < ?

The analysts don't count this up. They seek the shortest way
and watch the money blink across the globe.
It comes home safe, folded many times,
and seems somehow to wink when passing by.

The Prims

Here the helpless, hapless, feckless commonage
in congregation on a May weekend at Mow Cop
to hear Hugh Bourne, who, even when speaking to thousands,
could not help but hold a shy hand before his face.

He carts the gospel from place to place, the word
of some god who is not Mammon and who likes the meek.
Who shall inherit. Inherit what? This show below?
potbanks, coal-smoke, salt-fogs, pit-heaps, saffrucks, soot?

These 'dear peculiar people' are not that daft.
They do not expect owt builded here to go up quick.
All they ask, free and familiar, is how to be
a worthy soul, and that their works shall follow them.

Thus Hon Treas., always in his best on Sundays,
rattles year by year his tin of cooperation.
It will add up, even though only copper, into a benefit,
a grand word and a grand thing: all do give so all may live.

Thus Hon Sec. reads the notices for the week, the rotas
and the tasks of patience. She knows that 'e'en the smallest thing
can do some good and comfort bring' and will keep at it,
entering in the minute-book the measures of their joy.

They gave their mite, these ranting Primitives,
a-shivering and a-shaking (agitating!) all through Sunday night.
Filled from the loving-cup, they descend lit-up into the dark.
May those who mock thee learn the dignity of love.

Manchukuo

1.

In a garden in Sawtell,
a black butterfly, gold-tipped,
jinks along a line of trees,
over the ferns and on
among the paper-barks.
On the creek two ducks appear
and disappear; purple blooms
waver in the stream
as though on strings;
the house-shadows
adjust their geometries.
By this time the creek
will be moving seaward –
will be, as that fly,
in the same divisible time
as the whip-bird's shout,
stands on the rim of a glass,
the water-dragon
takes a step,
and we carry forwards
what we have.

2.

What do I carry now
of Sandford Hill?
(*Local pronunc.* Sanfa-dill.)
I am trying.
Gaps of memory seem
another failing,

even another guilt.
There is the arch
leading into the old cartway,
the backs with their rough cobbles.
I can't remember its
leading anywhere,
nor where my mind went
in those child-hours
of afternoons out there,
under the arch,
by a few yards of wall,
a few flights of brick,
each brick nose to nose,
a different oblong:
this one wafering
revealing its inmost tangerine,
still a lick of whitewash
about another, several soot-veined,
each one's abrasion different
to the heel of a hand
as I seek the unseen glow
of the baker's wall,
warm from the morning
and still proffered, as,
outside the arch,
the day tightens and withdraws.

3.

The true date
of the start of World War II,
this historian says,
was September 18th 1931.
This was the day
the Empire of Japan,
in becoming the Empire

to vanquish Empires,
invaded / liberated
Manchuria / Manchukuo.

Is the historian right or wrong?
I do not know.
I do know that there,
in the grandeur of time,
someone was sitting in a garden,
someone was gazing at a wall
and were caught up,
made a part, fitted in,
and I think we should try
to understand the flow, the sweep –

Perce, my uncle,
who died of that war,
in some moment of that day,
September 18th 1931,
almost surely,
passed under the arch,
perhaps brushed his coat-shoulder
against the brick
as he swung out into the street.
I imagine him 'swinging'
because he was only ever young
and I have little else to go on,
little to describe,
though I can invent whistling,
boys whistled then.

And as he 'swung out' the last time,
brushing his greatcoat
against the brick,
his kitbag on that shoulder,
perhaps he put his hand to the wall –

But this is harder to research
than the Nine Powers Treaty
the Peace of Paris,
the Washington Conference,
the League of Nations,
the Kwantung Army...

Like those of other polities,
Perce was moving seaward,
carrying forward what he had,
past the arch,
through places –
Malaya, Malacca –
I might just imagine,
to a moment which,
with nothing to go on,
I can neither know
nor conjure.

Sunday Afternoon

Will Heath, never good on his feet,
turned the corner from Chapel
one smokeless Sunday afternoon,
tippling a little, unjustly, as though
his Sabbath boots were welted with the weekday clay,
and, though always slower still of speech,
often malapropic, was eager with words for me.

He smiled and put forth both his hands.
'Look thee,' he said, and on one palm he held
a box of fire-brick and within it a nest of flame,
and in the other hand a jug, of yellow earthenware,
filled with water to the brim.
'What hast thou got there?' I asked him.

'Look, this is the fire,' he said, 'that can burn Paradise,
and this the water to douse the flames of Hell.
Then all on us will love the Lord
not for our reward, and not for fear on Him,
but for His Own Sake.'

I love thee Will Heath,
but fled the one Sunday afternoon
I did spend in your Sunday School,
put there that through the tall, colourless windows
faith might strike the child.
On the cold bench, odorous with wax and incorrupt,
I sat unstultified,
not lifted up by the pure and empty light,
nor by the men bellowing at hymns,
released as they were from something,
their sins they would say, the father's strap still lingering,
released as they were and recognized –

I love thee Will Heath
and sorrow too for your long, patient widowhood
spent by the kitchen table,
the oilcloth always well wiped down;
your every place of worship closed one by one,
even the red tin tabernacle on worthless ground,
till you were homeless.

And if I met you again in the street,
or cutting across the waste, or wherever,
I would stop you for sure and ask you
how it went with the water and the fire,
and I would hope you would say: 'They are consumed.'
And then I would ask that you take me and show me
the dwelling of such selflessness and unassuming,
and this Lord that you have made.

Agricola

agricola: a word
like shards
cutting the palm,
pieces of the stone sun
re-made in travertine

.

agricola: a response,
a riposte to the earth,
human work

.

much to do with beating:
the near-off clash
of wood and metal,
a knot struck,
the spittle of
hammer-flaw

.

a fork
in the curved track
that keeps on curving,
the widening space between
fitted up with jottings
of bushes and small trees
before the strange wood
and its deep trees

.

all morning
traction through vetches
and horse-corn, once bull-dragged;
at length some polished furrows

•

tanks in fields
for water or fuel oil;
other containers
improvised,
white bath tubs
with tide-lines,
phosphoric green

•

banished machinery,
clustered, rusting together,
better than gawky
some loaders heron-like

•

harrows untoothed,
ploughshares broken on stone
will not go unvisited:
the tinkerers come here daily
to seek a strut, bolt or chain
to use or save

•

in his pound
the sculptor Smith kept a troop of
old spaders, ridgers,
wagons, winnowers

to climb among, dismember,
and then hammer
to something new

•

corrosion:
barrel-hoops,
a garden fork, prongs only,
a mattock head
shaped like a face

•

grease for
bolts and hinges,
malt-brown with
white peaks standing
as the fingers leave it

•

a bunch
of lavender is drying,
hung like a totem sheaf

•

the shed,
its oils, creosote,
dust-gloves, raffia,
nail-box, screw-box,
the rake, the fork, the spade

•

those bloody
nasturtiums in the

cinder-soil
untidy and ungrowing

•

scratty fruit-canes
gone wild, dens and scabs,
coltsfoot is nearly pretty;
fustian dock good medicine
bound on to nettle stings

•

the road to
Rhayader logged
then mined long ago;
the grey spoil-screes,
the head-gear,
its red flaking slowly
into the air

•

hammering again,
now further off;
something is being changed

•

a hot afternoon
and a low ceiling,
a brown strip of paper
uncurling downwards
weighted with flies;
the strange fleecy peach
offered as a treat

•

stench of fern-coverts,
rabbit-droppings look
like currants;
fern-days of purposeless
hiding

•

waste-ground,
whatever margins and
fents of land not built on,
sometimes pasture
for a rag-and-bone piebald

•

on one side
rough grass too steep,
on the other
coal-scree
useless slack
and rubble

•

further round
more spoil, the saffruck,
white crocks
underfoot, sliding
this way and that

•

Agricola
marches upon
the Black Hills
and the Lion's Head;

comes home
'black as the road',
the enemy, unengaged,
'melted away'

•

across the waste,
Peter off the lead
and at once about
the stubborn grasses
the scratched tilth
of clinker and potsherds

•

grasses torn off
for the clay beneath,
white and sopping,
draining on to lorry wheels
spattling the roadway

•

pigeon lofts
furnished from wardrobes,
cupboard sides and shelves,
the fowl roosting
among cup-hooks,
job-lot paint stripes
to bring the birds home

•

old tank containers
sheared down at the corners

and unfolded
like a blown tulip

    •

other lean-tos,
a cross-and-bible door
laid on its side,
blue-grey corrugated,
its bolt-holes black or rust-fringed

    •

by the gate
tied with orange twine,
the deep-pocketed sludge
under the beasts' feet

    •

besides the rough-tough cabbage
hefty potatoes
and bantams scratching,
a farm of coal-picking
and even mining, the seams
slanted into the hill

    •

the last tak'in of the fell
yielded winter pasture
though stumbling ground;
the grey-white, pieced
and mounded walls
loosen, the falls strung with wire,
some trodden down of course

•

lawns obligatory:
the seeded area
with criss-cross hairs
fluttering with foil
and rags to serve
against birds,
like a pair of trousers
flap-hanging in a tree

•

lawns obligatory:
swiss-roll turves
with all herbage pared
and relaid –
it's the smart answer

•

aubretia
on its rocky islets
of broken quartz,
cascades white and purple
by front paths and drives,
always much admired
of a summer Sunday
at eventide

•

how well
can be known
an unmade road:
the quartz grains,
cinder glints,

the dull shine of tar-lumps,
each rain-puddle
re-finding its old shape
and depth

.

canal-making
with a beat-up soup spoon
tarnished yellow
but serviceable,
small dams and atolls

.

verandas
always in peril
creepers waving to get hold;
saplings urged upwards

.

the small plum
was split and leans
helplessly; just in
this light, this morning,
its fruit, known
to be purple
is nearly as white
as the stones

.

a quarry
as though one hand
has opened the earth

so talc can be
trundled away
and golden gravel
sieved and washed

•

Agricola: the earth scratched
for a living

These Things

'But Nature is a stranger yet'

EMILY DICKINSON

Flowers that do not look brisk –
sharp, upright, attentive –
but are always unkempt, dishevelled,
whether in spring-yellow or mourning purples,
seemingly fatigued, distracted,
they care not, but get on as well as better.

And these other creatures at their work,
fond marigolds, that strangely pinkish tree,
a long list of insects, never reposeful,
a bird staying hidden, its song inscrutable,
none of these things is singing or smiling our way.

•

Here, by a complicated tree,
among a few stones, that, as ever,
gaze only at the ground, I am on watch.
Two bright flowers are splashed nearby,
otherwise all is green – or greens –
save the grey tatters of the tree-bark.
A magpie introduces his black and white
and swaggers it around.

Green, grey, black, white,
not much 'claptrap of colour' here.

•

The creek is slowing as it draws to turn.
A tree, grown out over the water
has taken its chance to head upward for the light.
Like the wind, light makes its own alterations
and is different again from the waters'
punctual beck and call.

This much is going on, as we say,
or whether we say it or not.
What is this business of saying?
(It is time I could say something.)

•

Rain today. It brings its own changes:
the bark is darkened, there are glints on leaves,
the creek is spattered.

Below the notch in the tree,
the grey in the bark now looks like tar
clawed downwards across the pale ground.

Heedless, even nerveless, the bush-turkey
checks back and forth across his ground,
his gold throat shuttling up and down.

Warm enough now, the cicadas give tongue,
and a lizard is out on a branch,
monument-still for an hour,
silvery and green. Smart as paint he is.

•

Leaves on the creek demonstrate its flow.
They are like a small fleet, each moving
as though seeking station for convoy onwards.

Then there is the current itself to be seen
ridging the water.
It quickens and then canters inland,
carrying the correct volume and movement for the day
as though it understands itself.

I am on watch.
What might drop from the roof?

•

A sudden whistling in my ear,
a jasmine star with its five points,
the clank of a workman's tools dropped,
the sweepings of the pavement,
leaves and the clatter of leaves,
the rose, upright, noble,
the faint tracery of a tall grass.

I am not going far for these –
I can look, listen and find them.
They seem to be things that I know.

My ear whistles at me,
the five hearts of the jasmine flower,
the brief shout of metal on paving stone,
leaves and litter blown together
and swept across to be shovelled,
the rose also inclined,
the fawn grass melting away.

I am attending
but they are what they seem to be,
as Fernando said
(not his real name).

•

(Elsewhere)

Walking the beach, the wind at our back,
sand-skim rushes before us,
it twirls and eddies,
more erratic than a flock or shoal,
though doubtless there is a rule.

Undisturbed yet, the casts of sand-crabs,
patterned like chase-work,
each copiously and differently done,
might be said to decorate the scene,
each tight drill downwards casually enhanced.

·

I am on watch.
I stoop to the ground:
there is no echo of itself.

There are these things and sometimes the shadow of these things
but they will not be seen apart.

The pansies in their two colours at my feet –
two purples – keep themselves to themselves.

All I see is time and what might be like and like,
the watch-winding cicadas for instance.
I fear these things are no more than they appear to be.

Predictable Days

If the day predicted falls out
as it should and the small hawk
arrives on its noonday
draft of air and works lazily

across the hill,
and the wind rises in the afternoon,
and the white rock clings
to the light deep into dusk

then time will have passed,
some time will have passed,
and no offence taken,
only its customary tribute.

I like predictable days,
baffled by no more than a sun dapple.
Mystery, the glamorous chaos-engine,
breaks things, lives included.

Passing

The scrape of a spade
on a paving stone.
An arena of light
on the yellow grass.

The spade keeps working –
something is being made.
The arena widens
as the shadows retire.

It's all change and change-about,
coming and going,
a distant hammering takes up,
then a mattock at the ground, *tac tac*.

I'm feeling carried along –
will nothing pause?
Can nothing arrest itself?
Can no one see this passing?

Shading In

A sea-fret might be shaded in,
but then, the sun,
as though uncovering a tureen,
has it vanish quite away.

Vanish – though such a fret can return
stealing. . . but what is it stealing?
It is not furtive, or embarrassed,
it simply shows itself

without any purpose –
it cannot be said to know purpose.
But I cannot let it just
show itself: I must nail and nail,

making it, for example, into a salute. . .
And the line ends just there.
That tureen now,
was it patterned or was it plain?

Self-Portrait

After R. B. Kitaj

Did you laugh so, so late?
Was your beard so red, so long?
Were you by then, or always, a Dodgers fan,
or is that cap a prop just come to hand?

By what right do I ask you these things?
And use 'you' so familiarly,
you whom I never met
or even saw or heard, in the flesh?

Is it because one feels one can take liberties
with the dead, as with the slightly famous
who can be papped in supermarkets
or accosted in the common street?

Are self-portraits everyone's property?
have you given yourself up to one and all,
and all who look are worthy
and free to take what they want?

I want that blue cap and orangutan beard,
things I think I can get away with
in this mood for picture-making.
Should you have been so generous?

An Empty Street

after Ottone Rosai, via San Leonardo

What is there to an empty street?
And one so commonplace,
narrow, with two high walls,
bending out of view.
No one in sight
and no one expected.
No Dame Trot for sure,
with her basket over her arm,
the check cloth covering dainties,
her hat perched so,
her pince-nez expectant.
Even she has hurried away.

•

What is there to an empty street?
The photo (bottom right,
curated later)
shows the doorway
to have been your studio
(there's a plaque).
Still no one to see.
Have they tiptoed round
another way, anxious
to preserve its vacancy for you
and leave your lines,
so carefully set forth, intact?

•

What is there to an empty street?
Let's get impatient,
let's add a soundtrack
somewhere beyond
but coming on this way.
We'll have a marching band,
cornets, clarinet
and big bass drum,
at least the air is moving!
Until we lose control –
the band has wheeled away.
You, or the street, has won again.

·

What is there to an empty street?
Have you seized it
for your melancholy,
shushed and deterred
all would-be passers-by,
your neighbours,
even understanding friends,
emptied them out
like plums from a paper bag
and then folded
and re-creased it
as you have it now?

·

What is there to an empty street
that you will not let it go?
There is no blood,
robbery or impiety
open to the view,
no spectacles required
to see what can be seen,

not even, for certain,
what I've called your melancholy.
So you leave me here,
just as you meant to do,
watching the street.

·

What is there to an empty street?
Is it one of those secret worlds
with metaphysics skulking in the walls,
that door so enigmatic?
Maybe there is something
we might wish to see
face to face, to be
chased from the shadows,
or shaken from the trees
but we never –
These workaday walls are still
the only splendour to be seen.

·

What is there to an empty street?
This time there is a tree,
like a fright wig,
looming above the wall.
The street is embarrassed,
the wall hides itself in shadow,
the corner beetles off
to its secret lodging.
The tree allows two points
of light, like puppets' eyes,
to hold and behold
the bluish scene.

·

What is there to an empty street?
Almost nothing now:
The red wall
the grey wall
the yellow road,
green trees, the blue
of the sky, all simplified,
all still obdurate,
still resisting,
still insisting
they not be named
wall, road, trees, sky.

•

What is there to an empty street?
It seems all that remains.
The corner turns
into the unglimpsed
and none has passed by,
it seems, in ages.
But thus far the walls
and even the trees,
for all their skittering,
appear dependable.
They will not fly off, by Jove,
and leave us darkling.

•

What is there to an empty street?
To be candid now
the terror that it not be there.
Already so much particular
is gone, chased away
by the rage we find
for order: the simply sunlit,

the clearly pure,
the assent to less.
You must have seen it going
before your very eyes,
but you painted on.

                 •

What is there to an empty street
and yet how easily
I find myself enticed
along your unfathomed carriageway.
And isn't this
what you made it for?
You paint no footfall
but I can hear my steps
and the rustle of my clothes
as I proceed along,
sidling sometimes to pass through
the viewless crowd.

                 •

What is there to an empty street?
With this one there is the future
possibly, which is always
curving out of sight,
naturally. Out of sight.
But no one wants to see it,
which is why you are alone
and invisible, save for what you see,
what you can't help but see:
the thickening light,
and whoever has gone before
and had to leave you here.

                 •

What is there to an empty street?
The bruise of the dark corner
as it fades,
the antiquity
of your painstaking lines,
verticals and horizontals,
such composure –
Nice, but how I'd love to drive
a barrel hoop
down your street,
ruddy and exulting,
a boy of nine again.

•

What is there to an empty street?
Well, look hard enough,
tap-tap at it,
wait by the gate,
peer at the tree,
meditate upon the bend,
walk the footpath
back and forth
and patience
will recognise your diligence.
And as the street dissolves
you shall be beckoned.

•

What is there to an empty street?
Do not break your nails
striving to climb the wall,
do not beat upon the gate
and you will flounder
if you try to pass the bend.
Pinch yourself:

this is where you are,
plump and slow.
There is no casement,
enchanted cleft or chasm.
Nowhere to pass or tumble to.

·

What is there to an empty street?
Might it as well be
dead nature,
like a glass of juice,
a cherry and its shadow,
sometimes a cruet?
Dead nature
with its auspices,
even the tree is
motionless and dumb.
Look how stock-still
you will come to be.

·

What is there to an empty street?
But I am drawn to it,
indeed I fall upon it,
it saves me
from looking elsewhere,
saves me from knowledge.
Yes, it will do,
it is as much as I can deal with.
No pundits here,
no hucksters
touting
the difficult future.

·

What is there to an empty street,
as empty as an afternoon,
paused in summer?
Only you are awake
to look at it,
always vigilant,
like the master
standing above his pupil.
Is this it?
Just as you want it?
But that cooking smell,
how long can you bear it?

•

What is there to an empty street?
The relief from indoors,
from what is behind the white gate,
inside the dull windows:
three men in hats
cheating each other at cards;
another solemn *concertino*;
a man on his haunches
with his face in his hands,
others whispering.
It is not free out here,
or genial, only quiet.

•

What is there to an empty street?
Suddenly I notice a lilac tree
spilling over the wall
just in sight, before the bend.
Or it could be plums
so prolific they colour out
the leaves.

How did I not register
so much activity,
the purpling underneath the window,
the purpling sunset
of the waiting storm?

The Nearly Empty Street

After Ottone Rosai, via San Leonardo

This is that nearly empty street
breathing in real life.
Should I be surprised
I can find that tree,
the doorway
– both trees –
the lilac and the pine?
How faithful you were,
how devoted to what you saw!
Two funeral cars speed away
disappearing fast,
their office done.

.

This is that nearly empty street:
a parked car
and someone locking it.
A workman's wagon,
drives from your door
plaster-spattered,
step-ladders, trestles,
tubs of paint aboard,
the door left ajar.
This is time, movement,
alteration, your house
not now as you knew it

.

This is that nearly empty street,
changed also
at every moment
by our idling along.
The church porch
stands open to the light and air
of noon, the door-curtain
billowing suddenly.
Here is a secret world
for sure - in those
billows, their restless shapes
promising and concealing.

•

This is that nearly empty street
where sun and earth collude
and the shadows
are for real.
The stone dog thinks
that it commands its own
but look how faint
its image is
cast across the ground,
how frail the tree branch
striving on the wall
but losing itself.

•

For this moment the street is empty,
no *motorino*,
no passer-by,
and we have caught it thus.
The olives on the right
pour shadow
across the paving stones.

The foreground wall
bears all the detail
of abrasion, flake and crack.
Just now, the bend ahead
we can forget.

•

Captured on this nearly empty street
a plastic sack,
packed and tied,
and placed neatly
against the wall
but precious little else
unless, pressing the zoom,
that is a small gate
down to the right
that I might be able,
all unseen,
to slip inside.

•

This is that nearly empty street
teaching me what I can see:
the brass clasps
of some scaffolding;
a circle featured
in the streetlamp's fixings;
one louvred shutter
open at right-angles to the wall;
the stone lion on the gatepost
has graven furrows on his brow,
no bravado –
his moustache almost comic.

•

What there was to your empty street
– I can see it now –
did not rely on shutter speed.
As you painted
your whiskers grew
your stomach rumbled
perhaps your fingers
grew stiffer than they were
and liver spots appeared.
But your street stopped
all that dead.
The paint is motionless.

        •

This is that nearly empty street
and we are happy here.
We could do handsprings,
skip rope,
play tick,
anything as long as
we watch for traffic.
This really is *the real world*,
as it is always known:
we got off the bus
just there at the top of the street
and that proves it so.

        •

This is the nearly empty street
of the here and now
where parking restrictions
must apply,
messages overfly
and dancing on the spot
becomes obligatory.

Ah this self-excited present,
lulled by its eagerness
not to notice
the tow always underway
out of it.

•

This is that nearly empty street
which can ignore
passages not its own
but still only feign
time cancelled,
or its flow forgotten,
as when we grasp
one moment
of unshadowed joy
and feel the future cannot come,
or at least pretend
its step cannot be heard.

•

Along this nearly empty street
we amble from side to side –
the wet paw-prints
of a curious dog
along a path
could be ours.
There's nothing to speed us,
not the interesting arch
that is
– must I say *is*? –
at the bottom of the street,
or up to now is said to be.

•

This is that nearly empty street.
Does it make you laugh
to watch me treat it
like a metaphor,
that just because
you painted it shut
leaving your meanings
so far inside what seems
without consequence,
I turn up on 'the street itself'
as though my blunt blade
could break the seal?

·

This nearly is 'the street itself',
though what it is
remains still
uncertain yet.
Is it Rosai's mind
painted on out there
or is it the wall
I'm pressed against
as a van comes by?
Is it profitable
to decide on which?
Give me life and give me art.

·

This is that nearly empty street.
However happy-go-lucky
we feel, however
embarrassed the street appears,
it still has our measure.
Its bends beckon us on
not urgently, not insistently,

and only to reveal
nothing much yet,
no smile sinister.
But I look for a bench or a stool
to pause upon.

•

This is that nearly empty street.
Though it looks as it does
it cannot stand still –
there is a car slowing down,
workmen going off for lunch,
whatever moves,
us.
The stone dog and stone lion
show us nothing,
they are all sham,
pretenders, deceivers,
mockers, smirkers.

•

This is that nearly empty street
you had me watching
and which now I am walking on,
cannot help but walk
in the sunshine.
That it is congenial
cannot be denied,
though why might anyone
want to deny such a thing
as sunshine,
a pleasant walk,
life indeed, as it walks.

•

This is that nearly empty street.
I could turn back
but where would
that get me to?
Another street,
but still walking,
gait just the same
though a limp might set in
and I might want to stop.
But even if it takes a litter,
I shall be lifted
and carried forth.

•

This is that nearly empty street
and what is there to it?
Thank you Signore Rosai,
your truly empty street
truly entertained me
and I am grateful for it.
But of course I must walk on,
check the guides again
regarding
that interesting arch,
though I'll still be surprised
to find myself there.

•

This is that nearly empty street
that we have come to see,
nondescript as it is.
We are continuing
our walk,
crossing from side
to side, pausing

conversing,
the three of us together,
merry enough,
and the fourth of us
up in front and now out of sight.

Clouds

Here is some time not headlong
but which is just now, quite early morning
when the cloud below us,
but above the lake,
stands in the sun
though just moving, as if herded,
in this case northwards
no commotion.

Nothing is more pacific it seems,
nothing more at ease, not resigned,
at ease,
even as it is carded
and pieced apart
stretched out and combed
as the sun steadily
warms the air.

This going it abides,
no demurral, no recoil
and what that would imply
for time,
until the last wisp possible
is led aside
out of appearance
lost and content.

•

The clouds are to be envied,
did I make that clear?
They are composed,
strangers to anguish,
they accept what comes,
they will not rail
uselessly
rending and howling.

They do not mind
that they will not come again,
the molecules of another day
will belong to that other day
to what this patch
of earth and air
makes up
according to the rule.

Do I make this clear?
Then why, you ought to ask,
should human habit
be so dispraised?
Do we imagine dignity
to give it to a cloud?
Do we imagine questions
to admire what must stay mute?

•

Mute the nature
we always turn to
that has no manners
that does what it does
and fair enough,
so benign the dog-rose
so languid the moon
we are embarrassed.

How have they learned
there is no use in worrying
it never is worthwhile
when it is the while
dawn to dusk, upsets us?
We are the ones who know
the cloud and flower
decease, and it is

their grand indifference,
their immunity to sadness
and to scorn we laud.
Our mind is the stranger here
always ill-at-ease,
always envying
never content to be
the kind of thing it is.

My Childhood

In the sound of my pencil
my childhood. It is everywhere
nowadays, like a not unfriendly
scratch, a pin-prick archipelago.

It seems eminently treatable.
Could it even disappear?
A dab of peroxide and cotton-wool
and a little more time again.

But no, it will not depart,
indeed it detains me,
like an arm in a sling,
a leaf blown into a corner.

But that is not truly how it is.
My little childhood plays a merry game
as though still out on our street,
but sees it policy to let me be.

On the Grass

'I do not see us reabsorbed into nature.'

GEOFFREY HILL, *ODI BARBARE XLV*

I *do* see us this way, or have seen, perhaps see,
no, do see.

See what I have done: I threw my parents' ashes out together
on the grass.

There they would be suffused, blown off, well soaked
and damped in.

And I thought this is not only decent, civil, and
well sanctioned,

but as apt as can be, for this garden, though planted out and
duly mown,

the modern woodland walk titivated and
neatly stepped,

is still kin to those haphazard stars whose hearths will
welcome them.

As we go, here we come, dust-risen, new things re-
organised,

by strange remembrance made and then quickly into
unmaking,

embraced by the wasp's salivered clay, or fire-damp, or
fennel seed.

•

And how restful this promise to bring us home to
nothingness,

to be finished, accomplished, and without
remainder –

I do think I can see this. Yet it is somehow un-
satisfied,

this mind's eye. It was soon looking elsewhere,
its dumb lens

bumping the light, starting to spy itself, trying to
recognise

even one disinterested, helpful thought,
striving to

corner some faith in an unpainted bedroom at
dead of night,

learning how it is of some account,
curious,

unreconciled, keen to get somewhere at least
dignified.

It will die scrabbling. It wants to lift you
from the grass.

Both Sides

these are my parents
whom I know to be dead

yet here they are
at a distance waiting
squashed it seems
into a kiddie-car
gig or dog-cart
– it's hard to tell –
but in a holding pattern
and among the clouds
of course

and they seem composed
even smiling I think
though how can they like
where they are?

what would they want to see?

and on the other side
out of sight among the grass-trees
the as yet unborn
also waiting

To J. D.

'My dear friend nowhere in sight
This Han River keeps flowing east'

WANG WĒI, 'MOURNING MENG HAO-JAN'

1.

My dear friend, where are you now?
Nowhere in sight, not in your half-glasses,
nor turning a page, nor looking askance.

The right bus turns the corner and you get on,
and that's not to be seen again either,
nor your shopper's eye for rabbit-meat or veg.

The sands of Ynyslas, the tides of Forth,
stretch and flow, west and east.
Their inks touch-in the sky but show nothing.

2.

My dear friend, where are you now?
No sight nor sound, no hide nor hair,
nothing but imagined conversation.

A word on Vishnu of the thousand names perhaps –
stuff you knew about – and cool Krishna teaching
that pain is no more to be considered real

than sun, shadow, books, all the familiar clutter.
At the end I think you wanted rid, without
ever being persuaded you were lifted up.

3.

This is your dear and too-European friend asking
where are you now, now you are history,
(as they say)? 'Now' well defined as 'without you'.

As it did become, insistently, for you: *'without...*
without...' until time was no longer history
but held up its hands, unwrote itself,

renouncing pattern, promise, progress, novelty.
What I want now is you here with me
to discuss how that ever could be true.

4.

My dear friend, where are you now? Here I am,
away from your haunts, round the corner
from the sun, hiding from its havoc.

But there are tall, genial flowers here, even hollyhocks,
big sprightly daisies, packed in plots
as you would like, even if every one's an optimist,

and round them a lunkish, tar-black beetle
falls silent for each flower it reaches,
then mithers on. On. Nothing includes you now.

5.

My dear friend, where are you now?
Sometimes I glimpse you in the swagger-land
of dreams – a cut-throat with one fingerless hand

and a plastic sunflower whirring in the wind
trrrrr tick tick tick tick trrrrr...
and some rhubarb steaming.

For all our handsome ingenuity of being
and of mind, such milk-tooth edits
are still the most that's offered us.

6.

My dear friend, where are you now?
I'll be skittish and put you next to Queen
Victoria's Indo-Scottish lover Elphinstone

so you might suss the truth of that old tale;
or, more fittingly, beside your sober-sided forebears,
the missionaries who challenged Vishnu in his lair.

Those are 'the ranks of death' as once understood,
A billet for each deserving novice past the grave.
I would not wish you find yourself alone.

7.

My dear friend, where are you now?
I want to keep this going in imitation
of the industry that's all around:

the birds working the evening draughts,
the flies unfazed by walking upside down,
the mole and worm's unseen and sightless toil,

the snails, avoiding eggshells, seem heedless
and automative. But activity grasps at life
and makes a sort of tribute, not a mockery.

8.

My dear friend, where are you now?
Close enough to sniff, or sense that I am
getting sentimental? No, not that close

of course, but bugs and birds in verses such
as these, offered as companion souls,
would bring out the skeptic scold in you.

Most death has been untimely, miserable –
yours but one – and we want something we can
do about it. Sentiment strives to caulk the wound.

9.

My dear friend, where are you now?
Nowhere, I am sure, where you can see
how I am using you, cribbing you inside

these 9-by-9 lines, yet still faithful to
your taste for rabbit with mustard sauce –
your presence conjured as by a signature dish!

You kept respect, if little *goût*, for poetry,
but even I cannot believe that it can make you
walk and talk, or otherwise give life to thee.

10.

My dear friend, where are you now?
This is the tenth time of asking and enough.
It is a whole number and most complete:

the unit and the zero, what is and what is not.
You broke off and fell that way while
I am still standing, still the upright one,

still numbered, something before nothing
– until the flux resumes
and I will no longer press for where you are.

Note

'My dear friend nowhere in sight / This Han River keeps
flowing east': from David Hinton's translation of 'Mourning
Meng Hao-Jan' by Wang Wēi (701–761) in *Classical Chinese
Poetry: An Anthology* (2008).

The Immortals

Jupiter

O Jupiter, Lord of All as was –
Still just capable of turning over in your sleep
So we ask Grandpa what you said
As if you're still out there when we want to know:
Whom shall we turn to, to whom shall we turn?

But tonight I catch you when I'm caught short
Going home, caught short and whistling,
Gazing up over the rooftops and there you are,
Slightly tangerine, slightly flattened at the poles apparently
And in the telescope moons of your own
To rival the lady herself dropping a veil each night
And briefly you do seem Jupiter, 'stayer of rout',
'Giver of victory', *optimus maximus*, well worth
Your spec on the Capitol since pinched by Marcus Aurelius,
(Equestrian and bedside author, mere mortal).
Dux ductem ductis, boss, boss and boss,
Though where were you when tiny Mr Duffield,
Lost in the Gallic Wars, re-learned each day the savagery of boys?

And where are you now? Long descended from on high,
You're down the hill, elbows on the bar,
Nursing a beer they've named for you;
On good days spruce-ish, bow tie, toothbrush tash,
Button-holing as you detour to the Gents
Where you're gone an age, forehead on the cistern pipe,
Catarrah, yellow, heavy, won't drop from your lips,
Coaxing, squeezing –
You're the sky no longer and cannot show us round.
Just don't do that little dance, Dad –
Landlord will you see him alright?

Let's observe the decencies at least.
Hasn't he got a son somewhere down south?
A Science Park near Rickmansworth?
Some god of background radiation?

Venus

O Venus, rising from Lurline Bay,
Your one-piece just rolled down,
What is a boy to do but hang on your every word
And especially gesture?
Please come down the beach café.
If you're a photo-shoot I'll post my genes to you,
You're the stock I'd choose alright,
Or if I could give them to you tit-for-tat
How many times would be considered
Extraordinary? O Valeria, Amelia sweet Lianne,
Propitious Queens of Love, we could be at it
Lunch and dinner, feeling the universe move ever outward,
Always to origins not endings, bodies a-tumble,
Not cogitators' mind and soul (how's this for a line!)
O Venus I'm the one to move the earth with you,
Help you with your hawthorn hedges (half-run wild)
Your trodden mires, boot-dung,
Rich and claggy marls, sludge and colt's-foot,
The slopes of rubble that you've colonised,
Your haycocks, bullock pasture,
Jam jars full of spawn,
Your turbid rivers at the flood –
None of this moves but by your love!

    ·

And if Mars, that real glamour boy,
Skin buffed and glossed, hairless to the drapery-fold,
My best mate, can be drawn to drowse

On your divan leaving his
Lance and tin-hat for the kiddies,
A ribbon cupid-tied around your calves,
I'll not be jealous, I'll not be wronged or peevish,
Nor drunk-distressed, sitting among the ironing,
Steam and starch, cross-legged
Like a little drummer boy, not unreasonable
Though genuinely screwed, fucked over by the mind's
Sexual pawing – *what do you do with him?*
No, I'll not be jealous, for then the fire-step
Could be stood down, the sniper stretch and snooze,
The exhaust in the desert cool
Before the demon finds and enters it.
Soft skin, softly unslain, let him waste
His afternoon with you – hush, by love and reason
It seems that you have done it
And there is no other dream but this.

.

Until, the kiddies learn to dress by the left.
Then boot-blacking the balls of the weakest boy
Will be the least of it. Captain Penus,
When he wakes, sticks it to you once more up the arse
And leaves you to his squad – *by god you should've seen us –*
callow delving, womb-tearing, young boys somehow hating life.

.

And is that you wiping your mouth
Chugging on Listerine?
Black girl, fucked al fresco on a mattress
in the lay-by dawn till dusk,
International logistics.

.

I have nowhere to go, not my sister's,
And my arms are thin, look, so thin.

Venus, is that you now, can we dare give up on you?

When you totter by and your breathing's bad,
You think you won't go in for coffee,
And don't know what you'd do without TV
And wonder why girls now always show their chests,
We must hang on and hang on
To see one more day of us,
One more increment to our lives
If we can love each other.

Apollo

Now Apollo, we've not looked at you,
Which of course we can't and thus does your gaze
Make light the perfect metaphor.

Sunny Apollo,
I don't have your eye for stitching, style or shade.
I rose once to wedding-gloves of yellow kid
But I am no handsome *l'homme aux gants*.
You however were only ever once discomfited,
So the story goes, and by your prick of course,
Before reason, and you've long been above all that.
You have no dread of error, no more fear
Of losing an argument than losing a girl.
The white kine sponged down for you,
Trusting heifers lowing upwards to your brow
Are brought to their knees by the spreading springs
Mystified, noses drizzling blood, the finest voices,
Maidens, anointed worshippers.

Indifferent to gory plaudits,
You might turn your head but don't.

Once you were thought time-expired
When out of other blood came the word
That divinity was not a lordling such as you
But some man, skinny, a frowner, shadow-faced,
Eyes black as flies wont to be stapled, pierced,
Twisted by other men and not inscrutable
But ignobly crying out.
                              Yet as he stood up
and stepped forth, you assumed him without a blink.
His eyes became your eyes of flame,
His wormy pedestal your flawless porphyry,
And below who must be scourged is scourged.
When Regulus, eyelids excised, is turned
Towards you you will not avert your gaze.

The serpent's hymn of adoration says you see everything
And deceive us all – *in the sun dwells intellectual fire,*
What are its eyes?

So are you the One? The one living and True God,
Everlasting, without body, parts, or passions,
Infinite power... wisdom... goodness...
Maker... Preserver... super string...... theory of everything?
But we have been learning, Apollo,
We know you what you are.

Because we could not bear the justice of your gaze;
Because you would not blink for anyone;
Because, although you'd slip among us smiling,
Like all the gods you do not really care.
So although we know we will go down with you,
Huddled, glowering, finally chilled out,
How we would love to see you sucked in

And wasted, your light clawed
Back and back, unable to escape,
Dwarfed by degrees, your countenance
The splut of sulphur-springs until
The skull of Apollo enters its own darkness.

Is this peevish? Yes, but you will rise above it,
For it is you who taught us you will die.
Always the modern god, you've made your brain
Downloadable *gratis*,
And show us the idea that through
Many seeings there is one light
And brighter and brighter it will show everything,
Such are our eyes. You will show us everything
And deceive us all. How we sing in adoration,
How we adore the stitching and the shade.

To Himself

Dreams and systems; humble wishes;
myths that sustain because venerable;
even a walk along the promenade
might do, undertaken regularly.

The sea uprears and then falls back,
turns itself emerald as though auditioning
to be a paradigm, another helpful,
dainty stepper with no power

to explicate or recommend.
So why not fill the time available
as these tall pines have done,
and with no more intent than they?

In fact, dream not, wish not, obviously
believe not. Abandon even the promenade.
As the sea turns itself, strive to imagine
nothing that would stir or stand.

Acknowledgements

Thanks are due to the editors of the following publications, in which some of these poems first appeared: *Times Literary Supplement*, *PN Review*, *Poetry and Audience*, *Stand*, and *The Warwick Review*.